Black Mountain Home

Black Mountain Home

By David Kherdian

CASCADE PRESS

Cover illustration by Nonny Hogrogian

Second Edition published by Cascade Press under exclusive license from David Kherdian

Kherdian, David. Black Mountain Home.

Summary: Poet David Kherdian draws inspiration from the woods of Black Mountain, North Carolina as he vividly describes nature's raw pureness.

ISBN paperback 978-1-948730-08-2
ISBN hardcover 978-1-948730-09-9

Inquiries regarding permission or bulk printing requests should be sent to info@cascade.press

Visit us at www.cascade.press

For Haig

INTRODUCTION

Although people seem to play a small part in the quiet drama of this book, it is the spirit of the people here that emboldens each new day with grace, beauty, and quiet splendor, and the reason people flock here to vacation during the summer months.

The one-half mile walk around Lake Tomahawk is the heart that beats quietly over this town, the perfect introduction openly awaiting the newcomer, with its special atmosphere that blends, naturally and breathtakingly, with the surrounding mountains, green and openly inviting.

Nature originates, man imitates, and what willing actors they have easily become, with such an audacious script in hand, laid out to be taken in.

And if you are new here, you have your first sighting of a black bear to look forward to, along with birds in abundance, some so small you want to catch and hold them with a kiss; and then sighting the other winged beauties here, from hawks to herons to ducks and geese and butterflies, with other creatures both visible and hidden: foxes, deer, squirrels, and ranging over lawns and within the woods, cottontail rabbits.

It's all in this book, and in greater detail, with the joys I have received from everything seen, or wanting to be seen, that these poems have tried to convey.

LORDLY LOVE

The boy young man,
with shortened leg
walks slowly by,
open but alone,
a narrow
red bandana
across his brow

Arriving quietly here
at the shore of this pond
sized lake, to be
visited by flying ducks and geese
that leave or stay,
to be with him

Squatting crossed legged
to hold a wing hurt
Canadian goose,
in his grass grounded lap,
left behind when the other
honkers flew away.

They speak to each other
in the silent language
they share,
in stilled quiet,
in understanding love,
here in a space found
that found them,
for a love that is theirs
but not theirs alone or apart.

CONTENTS

BLACK MOUNTAIN

Clouds are different here—
abundant, in surround,
often sitting fatly on the horizon,
alone or not. Some days they
are the horizon.

Intimate clouds—like neighbors
or relatives, whether close up or
close by.
Their unfamiliar shapes soon to
become familiar—heedless,
unpossessed, divine.

Always completely themselves—
not wandering figments of
someone else's imagination,
but something almost ours;
and on days when they do not appear
we have our glorious North Carolina
blue sky—unlike any other ever seen before.
What joy, what easy surrender
to whatever life brings us now.

NEXT

The bears have their hibernation,
and so we have yet to spot them—
in particular that one who claims
this street as his own,
or so we've been told,
while less audaciously, flowering azaleas,
for whom this street is named—
as providential for us as our lone bear:
for we are newly arrived into this wonderland.

In our front yard stands a tall tulip tree.
Imagine!
If it were to all end right now, it will
have been a magical two months,
as is said of wondrous times and places after
whatever it was that made them such
fizzles back into the soil and sorrow of everyday
life—and always
with our breathless sigh, No Matter!

What *does* matter right now are the three
(not one or two) families of Canadian Geese,
in our tiny lake down the hill,
who are at peace and play with their
new sprung goslings, who are already
aggressive, reckless and fearless,

as if immune to bad luck and misfortune,
unlike us people beings, doomed
to the vagaries of war and weather
and psychotic politicians.

And here this briefly told tale must end—
to be resumed in five minutes
or less by another.
If only we were at home here on this globe,
above the rules set in the stone
on this great unknown boulder we cannot see
the inside of, but in whose embrace we abide,
and in which it is clear nothing dies,
but contrariwise continuously recurs
in unending return.

ON SEEING MY FIRST BLACK BEAR IN BLACK MOUNTAIN, NORTH CAROLINA

She came out of the hills on the
other side of the highway,
heading straight for the stream running
beside the outdoor restaurant we were
seated in with others.
Other worldly: large and soft and black

And more beautiful than anything
any of us had probably ever seen before,
maybe in all the time of our different
lives—thrilled by her simple magnificence—
a life completely real and true,
intrinsically alive and present in her
very own, unblemished environment

Unlike these disposable toys, us—
we standing there alert, magnetized,
in our wavering colors—quivering,
and gasping in awe with utter
amazement over something more
real than anything seen before

She rose up out of the stream and
sensing us nearby, quickly lumbered
off, a configuration of flawless grace

and indescribable beauty—
to disappear breathtakingly into a grove
of trees—her wilderness home.

SQUIRRELS

Busy early spring squirrel, jumping from
our dogwood tree to its large neighboring
tree, ran down, then back up—swiftly, swiftly,
take me home, its body quivered,
too much beauty here to own all alone—

Obviously needing company like our own next
door
neighbors, up a tree with illness—and like this
squirrel that we share together without
ownership,
wanting to understand the all of it,
as if any of it can be truly known to us—
innocent participants in the ritual and drama
of everyday life.

BLACK MOUNTAIN ARRIVAL

To live surrounded by woods,
alone but in their midst—
seemingly wild, seemingly untamed,
in what was once a lone valley
now shadowed by hillocks like
protruding breasts, named Seven Sisters

Black were the mountains when
we arrived at winter's end,
now greening in April,
what will May bring—

Flowers already in profusion—
up at the elder peaks,
brooding cousins patting
their nests
in the distant wilds.

BLACK MOUNTAIN RAIN

The rain when it falls on us here,
hurled down from Heaven on High—
in a thundering downpour, cleansing
everything at once,
a full-barrel bam-bam I'm the man—
not dainty and mincing, like rain very often
in northern cities on everyday streets
with regular gutters—but a drenching
full bore—over everything and everyone,
that even the trees love and welcome,
among tall grasses bordering newly sprung rivulets—
all of them happy, like an early release from school,
ever hoped for, to splash in puddles delicious,
the wonder of everything erupting at once—
with all the exploding parts suddenly at risk—
but then instantly the downpour stops,
with all the parts now rejoined and rejoicing,
free of taint, separation, and rust—
and at once instantly at rest.

NEW ARRIVALS

Here deep in the mountains
level spaces are treasured—
as sporadically found in our
conglomerate terrain of slopes
and slides and falls. But because of this
confluence
of unending configurations in the land,
there are often unusual surprises
and amazing delights—

For instance, there is now,
after a sudden thunderclap
and pouring rain, a rivulet—
rushing down the road
and making a gulley in front
of our driveway lawn—

That I have suspected would soon
bring arrivals of new life—
and for which we have silently withdrawn
watching and waiting for what might
emerge or appear before long,
more probably late at night—
suspecting at the very least to
see a frog or two in need of new
moisture, for what that might provide—

And so, eager to see if I am right,
I silently approach,
when at once a thin fleeting shadow
comes out of the stream
straight into the culvert
under our driveway, disappearing
in the still water holding there—

A miracle new home of safety and quiet
for these new renters has been made,
like us arrivals from outer space,
temporary squatters in their new home
on solid ground, water all around.

MORNING

We waken to dark ominous clouds
sitting atop our mountain close by,
as if they belonged there,
waiting to be dispersed and enlightened
by a rising sun that fires them
into glowing patterns

A silent action only light can make,
speaking to our temple carried within,
attuning us to something that is not ours
but that calls us to join

before all of it blows and
drifts apart and away
into configurations
for us to marvel upon.

JUST NOW

Just now the clouds crowning
the top of the mountain—
seen from our window,
have found each other

with a half-moon close by
in open daylight
observing itself in quiet.

HOUSE

All sides of the house
across the way
are unfamiliar with
one another,
as if each belonged
to another home
somewhere else,
while the dog in the backyard
on a roped stake, twirls
all out of place and space
no matter which way
he turns or runs,
while the squirrel
crossing the electric
wire above,
looks down
without stopping,
free of everything
even the sky

POEM CLOUD

This morning, looking out our window,
we were stunned by the sight of thin bands
of white clouds streaking over the mountain,
crossing over and under each other,
or dissecting into floating cubes,
making shapes similar in design
to abstract art, but without any apparent
meaning or purpose,
unlike abstract art that struggles to be
knowable, recognizable, and viewed
by others, as *their* abstractions struggle
to cross over into another realm,
unlike these natural formations
of clouds today
sailing effortlessly, profoundly alone,
and unnamed,
appearing and disappearing,
vaporous, timeless immortals
high up beyond us in the open air.

BIRDS

Two small birds thrashing under
the bush beside the stairs
of our mountain home—
so very busy, and so urgent,
as always with small birds—

But our business is to identify them
for we are newly arrived
to this tiny wonderland town,
and there is no excitement like
seeing unfamiliar birds—
and then finding their names in the bird
book purchased at Sassafras Bookstore.

It is as if the day
is hanging on our learning their names—
needing to preserve this moment
by stopping the current to name
a single riffle of its moving life.

WE'RE NEW HERE

Just now looking out the window
on this hot indoor day,
a bush or baby tree is having an attack
of internal combustion:
with all its leaves quivering at once
in a happy fit of happiness—
well why not—aren't there
just as likely
pleasurable disturbances in nature.

While the tree, neighborly beside
and above it
is as stillfull and quiet
as a hummingbird on a limb—

hoping it saw the same thing.
I mean, aren't we all in this dance together—
well
if we are, then take my hand.

Wait! I'll ask our neighbor what
this object of wonder is called
(he, who told us yesterday the tall
poplar in our yard, is a tulip tree).

Thank God for names, and that we
can stand with others and call out
to each other in our own quivering
and shaking ways—

GOSLINGS

What indeed are these goslings—
self-assured, sailing
gallantly between their
parents all in a row:
one, two, three, four, five,
careless and free, elegant
and proud, their natures
in full already, as if born
knowing who they are
and not needing, like us,
to call aloud—

Being complete, and free
of failure, gain or loss,
at home in their being,
something we cannot emulate:
this example of true freedom
that comes from knowing,
simply knowing, that one is alive.

BLUEGILLS NESTING

Bluegills are spawning now
below the path we follow
on our morning walks around
still and quiet Lake Tomahawk—

We stop to admire their fleeting forms
ranging over their circular beds,
like disks of moon—remembering that
they always spawn on one side or the other
of moon cycles,
something that we had to learn,
that they inherently know—

Peering down at them,
and not wanting to disturb this
invisible life of theirs
that continues in its way,
as do ours, and not so different after all.
.

NEW DANDELIONS

Could these be a second growth of dandelions,
or perhaps their cousins—but so small,
surrounded by long stalks,
or spikes of green,
from which tiny drops of yellow
flowering dandelions have suddenly
appeared, like sweet pigments of yellow
upon a green canvas, painterly,
all along this westerly bank
of the lake's quiet shore

To be plucked at hungrily by goslings,
led here by their honking parents,
another tiny
quickly enjoyed moment
for them and us.

NEIGHBORS

Walking across the lawn
late afternoon,
to look again at the newly formed rivulet
beneath the road at our lawn's edge,
I startled—and was startled by—
a red-shouldered hawk lately arrived,
to hunt this ground—

Rising up directly in front of me—
(how had I missed seeing him?)
to fly to a tree stump just yards away,
turning sideways to keep me in sight,
while holding still, aloof, unafraid.

And so—our company is expanding in this tiny plot
of ours: a rabbit and its new born bunny—lately
spotted,
and three tiny frogs, seen only in a flash,
that may soon come into view or not—
what city living in this place is like—
wilderness interrupted—without *its* being
interrupted by us.
What could be better?

RED-SHOULDERED HAWK

Just now I walked out the door
and into the driveway to see,
perched on the electric wire,
a hawk, oblivious of me,
at home here, as we would like to be
feeling his awareness of us,
unconcerned, high above me,
lofty in this space that we have in common,
at home here, naturally, as we are,
longingly—

Calling this new habitation our home,
attempting to fit ourselves within
its boundaries, while
absorbing all there is to see,
and hold inside our invisible world,
as private to us as this hawk's
visible world is familiar to him,
one of us forever in exile, the other
silently at home.

WHAT IS THE QUESTION

I just walked down to see the rivulet
between our lawn and the road,
hoping to alert a frog or two,
but for the first time
met with only silence.

Which means the hawk I accidentally
flushed the other day by the
newly formed rivulet
has made his catch, and why we've not
seen him since.

What is this need of ours
that wants to stay near life
in all its varying forms—
which has reminded me at this moment
how I liked to catch tadpoles, when I was not
much bigger than a tadpole myself.

We can never have enough of one another,
and even when we seek silence
and privacy, in our minds always,
living things like people strike back.

GREEN

What do these trees and dense
under and overgrowth
think of themselves—
their sheer abundance that surrounds
the all, like an overwhelming wreath,
unbound. What does it make of itself,
here in this endless silence,
disturbed only intermittently
by wind and rain; its
lavish indifference
and heavenly quiet,
grounded, fecund, growing un-
endingly, with no regard for self.

And we pass through it daily,
wishing an answer,
a voice to appear in a whisper
out of its world, alive, alone;
if this is the unrevealed soul of God,
what is man to answer?
But if a question: where
is the soul in man, that, too,
abides in silence, not seen,
sometimes spoken to
by what cannot answer,
alone in its greenness,
to answer for itself
as only it can.

WEEPING CHERRY

What about the tree on our side lawn,
unlike anything ever seen before, with
its low branch that bends, holding a long
cluster of leaves, separate and alone,
while above, other branches making clusters,
also drooping, to comingle like a family,
no longer separate but joined.

Who then took which from whom:
did we learn about families from trees,
or did we send this idea out to them?
No matter, nature has its reasons and seasons,
also not unlike ours. Let it stand.

SOMEHOW

Somehow we have found ourselves
in this place of enchantment,
at home with all that surrounds us:

plants, trees, animals, the ever present
birds, here in body and song,
in flight or at rest

throbbing, chirping, our eternal delights,
along with heaving trees everywhere,
brush and bushes of every kind

and just below a tiny wildlife lake,
set in a bowl—our singular meadow,
beneath green mountains above

and inside all this we abide
with all that was here long
before, forever certain

everything around us
ever in movement,
growing in ways not for us to see,

essential for our Being, we sojourner
humans, lately arrived,
to transform energies for our planet's needs

all beyond our knowing,
while our own Being in embryo succeeds
or fails to grow in its own mysterious time.

HOMAGE

I miss the frogs taken
by the hawk.
Being so small and swift,
we never got more than
a glimpse of them—
darting away
at our approach,
back into the culvert
and out of sight.

Somehow all at once the balance
of nature seems distorted,
or could it be that I am
incapable of seeing the all as one,
believing that what was taken
is gone, while nature in its essence
remains undisturbed,
its breath unaltered its rhythm unrocked,
but going on, as I must,
another particle stirred in the mist,
ever seeking balance and rest and oneness.

PORCH HUTCH RABBIT HAVEN

The rabbit we spied in our backyard
at the end of March, shortly after we
moved in, must be the mama
of the bunny we saw the other day
on our lawn—and then, just now, a smaller
one appeared at the top of the stairs leading to our porch,
with another earlier, dashing out of the bush
at the bottom of the stairs—when I walked
out to have a look around.

Apparently, they have made a home
of sorts under our porch. Cottontail rabbits.
How special is that! With all the wilderness
about they have chosen the safe cover
of a place that humans made, a hollowed out
harbor of safety and comfort, I guess.
Well, aren't we the same, inside this
new dwelling of ours, unconditionally
free for them.

Hurrah!

THE LAKE

The fisherfolks, generally little boys,
come sporadically with their twitching rods,
absorbed as casually as all the others
who sit the benches or inside the one gazebo,
while others quietly walk or run
in the open air, a daily ritual:
slowly or swiftly circumnavigating
this tiny globe of water that is ours
and nature's own; its wildlife, like us,
tamed by the serenity of surrounding hills,
that hold us together in quiet day time
light awaiting the sublimity of dusk.

WINGS

Birds are the canopy
that wingingly sews
the sky and us into place,
all of it collapsible if not held
together by their continuous flight:
to fall apart should they ever depart.

How important is motion,
the flow in tapestries
seen only with clear eyes,
for a splendor always there
before us, not to be defined,
but to worship quietly:
we the wingless
our eyes to the sky.

OUR POND LIKE LAKE

The bowl our lake rests upon
within these surrounding hills,
has become an eye that takes
us all in—silent, self-possessed,
like us at the command of wind,
rain and sun and cold—

to quietly serve the wildlife within,
with those that swim over its surface,
our tamable wild geese and ducks:
for while we circle the waters,
walking, they glide freely over
its surface to dwell at its edges,
to meet us at its shores, abiding
with us in a rhythm that is ours,
taming the wilds slowly civilizing us.

FRY

Today it was the swarms
of bullhead fry, appearing like
black underwater clouds in
our pond like lake, with swirling
clusters of them everywhere
along the banks

Watched by us, confused
by their sudden appearance,
puzzled and curious—
but the ducks and geese
blasé inhabitants
of this wonderland of ours

Go about their business,
knowing this is really
nothing very new.

WATERS

Our small lake or large pond called Tomahawk,
after the tallest of the Seven Sisters mountain peaks,
that can be viewed complete from its southern
end, where nothing is ever to be seen
on its surface but water birds, for
neither boats nor swimmers are allowed—

Which is our gift to this little island paradise,
where nothing appears to disturb its tranquility,
but for the anomalous fishermen—sometimes
noticed at its banks—being mostly children,
with rarely a fish in bucket or stringer;
these mild fishing invaders,
like ornaments along its banks,
their varying shapes and sizes
undisturbing its surface glamor,
so quiet, that rain drizzles
that come and go,
to fall on this lake, are only more water
falling on water.

I NEED

I need but this bird
on this bright sunny day
flying across the yard—
seen in a flash from our window,
enriching this moment, to prove again
that my world is in hand,

to know that if all I thought I needed were
to suddenly drop from my consciousness,
I could enter this moment as the God
of my life, to uphold it endearingly,
because life is no more or less than this,
a moment of luminous clarity
giving thanks for each instant of life.

WE, TOO, AND YOU

Although it feels natural,
it is certainly unusual to live so
very close to the creatures here,
for whom this place is home naturally,
as it is but customarily so for us—
and yet, with our clothed bodies,
our walking shoes, and very different voices—
usually subdued, as their voices
are very often not:

Geese that squawk, ducks that quack,
bears that lumber, not quietly,
and deer that sneak along, while mice squeal,
and chipmunks scamper quickly along,
silently but seen; for all together
we are enmeshed in a mysterious harmony,
conjoined by Nature, each and all
deliberately intent on entering
and living their own life.

TODAY

Only this—out of the hosta plant
at the bottom of our porch steps
that we had stepped across,
the cottontail rabbit jumped out,
then stopped after a few hops
to consider our counter stillness—

We watching, happy to see him
after his brief absence—
pleased as he doubtless was pleased
that we are not a danger for him.

And so together we shared in
this small happiness.
Thank you mother of earth and sky
for another day in the light.

LAUNCH ONE AND TWO

What we took to be a simple, flat open
space for launching boats, during
our walks around the lake,
was filled today—strikingly—
by a legion of ducks,
some launching, duck fashion,
with others jostling to join in,
while a third contingent blithely looked on,
not tipping their hands—or should
I say, wings—

And then, just minutes after, when we
looked back from our seat in the gazebo
(that we had been headed for, before the
ducks entered our life) there
to our surprise a red canoe-like boat
appeared, about to be launched
from that now deserted space—
and this was perfect—
a young freshly hatched couple,
(without feathers or wings, being human),
with a black dog between them,
its ears flapping in rhythm to the southern breeze,
with us watching, not far distant,
contentedly at home in our bleacher seats.

REACHING

Why are the trunks of trees
that surround us here—so
angular tall and bare,
tilting often in this
mountain landscape

ever growing upward,
with their bundled branches
and leaves reaching for
the sun—in need of light
and warmth and care

and with trunks to take them there,
(the two together making one)
and for their green leaves alone to
know God,
His glory to impart.

WORLDS
  after reading <u>Walden</u> by Henry Thoreau

In this little world I am now present in
with creatures and limbs of trees
and growing trunks, also creaturely—
until I feel myself one of them,
as tenuous and as solid by turns

that I wonder, suddenly—what life would
be if occupied altogether only by humans,
with their various lone constructions,
all of it inhibiting happiness
and the pleasures found here

minute by minute, full of impending
and ongoing life,
to realize that this: here, now,
is creation—and absent this,
man alone, stranded on earth,
would be a greater Hell than
what could be imagined—
where imagination would be
crushed also, and lost,
alongside all of life

THEIRS

On occasion when I walk out onto
the porch to see again our growing bunny
there, just below us, munching on grass,
I am struck at how his ears like twin spires
point to heaven, elongating his tiny face;
and amazing, too, is his watch on me,
not fearful, apparently, but alert—
and as I look down on him, endearingly,
for being natural and more certain in nature
than I—I who have marveled at how easy it is
here for both animals and man
to occupy this common terrain that we love
longingly, and as they do very simply—
for they are the environment,
in this home we have made here
to slowly grow comfortable in, but
that is not ours as it is theirs.

CIRCLING

Sitting in our tiny gazebo
at lakeside,
busy little birds
fill us with their
joyous play: zigging
zagging, twirling, and
zooming,
circling all about us
in blazing sunlight
on this sky blue day;
what joyous splendor
for them and for us.
Ah, but what are their names?

LAKESHORE DRAMA

We stop and stare at them:
Perhaps it's a play or rehearsal,
but without a director or script:
A Canadian Goose standing
between two clusters of ducks
on each side of him, who are
occupied privately with their
own thoughts and affairs, some
nestled, merged in the sand
upon this tiny weedless stretch
of our lake's quiet shore.

They are a sight:
the goose standing upright,
alert, considering the waters,
while we, a different breed, look
out at them, trying to understand
this unusual conjunction of
oddly joined birds, strangely
configured in a drama without
words or sound or possible script.

Yet wanting a meaning to somehow
appear within this tiny dollop of time,
to help us understand and make
sense of our own lives—their lives
being a mystery to everyone
but their own silent natures,
inside this Nature that governs us all.

SWALLOWTAIL BUTTERFLIES

From our very first walk around the lake
the Yellow Butterflies appeared on this
trail or pathway—long made by the happy
feet of those who daily walk here.

Yellow Butterflies, according to myth,
bring fun and excitement for those they
appear before, and so we eagerly look out
for them as they flit and dash about us,

Ever flying over, returning but never landing,
enjoying us in their own way, with us reciprocating
with pleasure, always,
starting up before us, from the very
first day of their awakening,
and every lucky day since,
to absorb their beautiful presence in our lives.

A CHIDING

I recalled just now, while reading
the Black Mountain News, that we had
earlier frightened our wild bunny rabbit
from out of the bushy hosta plant
at the bottom of our porch stairs.

The article in the News said that rabbits
like to feed on hosta plants,
which information coincided with
our chiding ourselves just yesterday
over putting out scraps for our little rabbit

And also the many birds, who often alight
on our front porch, to look out at the day;
as we do from our porch chairs, realizing clearly
that it is presumptuous to think they need
our help, here where they are at home,
and we but visiting neighbors, ardent
and temporary.

IN THE SHADE

While having my hair cut
and beard trimmed on our
shaded porch,
I studied, with poised comb
in hand—for Nonny to retrieve
at intervals for snipping—

A male cardinal alight from
an overhanging branch
onto our wide grassy lawn,
landing in the shadow of
the tree he had dropped from

Nimbly to walk the edge
of its perimeter of shade,
avoiding, apparently, the sun-
drenched glistening grass,
protecting himself by edging away
from its blazing heat

That finally, he stepped into,
for the next miniscule event in
his ever eager needy life,
bugs in the grass perhaps,
and so, that is where he lost me.
Class dismissed. I went inside.

POEM

Two small morsels just appeared
sailing through the air—a white
winged butterfly and a grasshopper
(the first seen here), and stepping
round my car in the driveway,
a chipmunk scurried urgently
along the fence row as I started
up the stairs, flushed suddenly
with life, needing for once
just light and air.

BALLET

Honkers with their grown goslings are gliding
in regal formation over our lake's glass-still
waters, on this early morning summer day—
an unbroken string in ordered formation

Seemingly propelled by another vision—
unseen, mysterious, like the transformed water
they float upon and over in this desired movement,
in its moment of time.

Their stately, elegant, and noble water ballet,
having been scored exclusively for these elite,
exalted beings—who only now reveal
what has been known to them all along.

To graciously display themselves,
not for others, but for their Maker,
who has not forgotten who they are,
and matches their silence with His own.

AGAIN

A thunder rumbles,
while far below
a somber quiet
takes hold;
a sacred silence
appears in peaceful
descension
surrounding an emptiness
awaiting whatever will come,
and we are here, silent, not
separate or different
from whatever is and to be.

TURTLES

Over in the southwest corner of this
man occupied, natural pond—
a spherical shaped island, maybe 20 feet
long, by 5 or 6 feet wide,
comprised entirely of wild grasses,
two very small trees, and boulders upon boulders
in varying sizes. A creation made by man
and nature, natural enough to be real,
but no less supernatural as everything else

found here, including the animals who stay or visit,
touched by powers not understood,
although poets must be allowed to discern
its hidden truths,
for each time I look upon this tiny island
and its arranged boulders,
a longing arises within me
to see a turtle or two perched there,
completing a picture very alive in my mind.

I want to see on ground or boulder
these turtles that I'm told are here—
to show their tiny faces and not remain aloof.

Dear turtles we need you. We do.
Your shape for form, as the trees for size,

the boulders for weight and solidity,
and the roaming geese and ducks
for their enduring grace
over these peaceful waters—everyone's lullaby.

HONKERS

So tame here, a honker,
just a moment ago,
while we were seated
in the gazebo by the lake,
walked in from out of
the surrounding grass,
unobtrusively,
and ignoring us entirely,
he began billing
between the cracks of the
wooden floor, for some
nourishment apparently,
a seeming wonder to us,
from our not seeing any life there,
but then isn't poetry also
a finding of the invisible
wherever, seen alone
by the sighted, who are
unafraid to look over
whatever they like,
as it is with this poet
for all of his life.

ALL BIRDS

If it weren't for these birds—
around, above and beside us,
where would we be—their
singing and endless winging
among the trees and open air,
upon the ground or out of sight,
filling the earth and its air with song,
that joyously unwinds in chirps
they alone understand—a music
sent out from themselves, an
angelic choir supporting their
existence and now ours,
a dream we take away, feeling again
sweetly alive; with a bird there,
just above us on a branch, looking down on life,
to say, come in.

HERE NOW

I would like to visit
every store and window
in this town,
the last station on the road,
as I would every stone
on this path,
every pebble along the way—
to where I am destined—

Hidden from me, allowing
the events in my Being
to prepare for the final door—
that will open only then
to more than chance,
the defining moment
before the next step
into another land.

ABOUT THE AUTHOR

David Kherdian is the author and editor of over seventy books, that include poetry, novels, memoirs, biographies, retellings, and children's books. His anthologies include *Beat Voices*, and three seminal works: *Down at the Santa Fe Depot: 20 Fresno Poets*, that inspired a series of regional anthologies, *Settling America: The Ethnic Expression of 14 Contemporary Poets*, and *Forgotten Bread: Armenian American Writers of the First Generation*. With his wife, two-time Caldecott Medalist, Nonny Hogrogian, they have published three small presses, and as editor / art director, three disparate journals: *Ararat: A Quarterly*, *Forkroads: A Journal of Ethnic-American Literature*, and *Stopinder: A Gurdjieff Journal for Our Time*. He has, with his presses, journal and anthologies, along with his own work, helped place ethnic writing into the canon of American literature.

His many awards include the Newbery Honor Book, The Friends of American Writers Award, the Boston Globe / Horn Book Award, the Jane Addams Award, a nomination for the American Book Award, and two lifetime achievement awards: The Emily Lee Award, and The Armenian Star Award. His translations and retellings include the Asian Classic: *Monkey: A Journey to the West*. An hour-long documentary of his poetry and life by filmmaker Jim Belleau was released in 1997, and can now be seen among his Youtube appearances.

Made in the USA
Middletown, DE
24 November 2019